No Regrets

Barbara A. Palmer

"And we know that all things work together for good to them that love God, to them who are the called according to His purpose."

Romans 8:28

No Regrets

Published by
Kingdom Kaught Publishing, LLC
Odenton, MD 21113 USA
Printed in the U.S.A.

Copyright © 2017 by Barbara A. Palmer

All rights reserved. No part of this book may be reproduced, stored in retrieval system, or transmitted in any form or by any means – electronic, mechanical, photocopy, recording, or otherwise – except for brief quotations in printed reviews, without written permission of the author.

Unless otherwise indicated, all Scripture quotations are taken from the King James Version of the Holy Bible. Scripture quotations noted The Message Bible are from The Message Bible, copyright © 1993, 1994, 1995, 1996, 2000, 2001, 2002. Used by permission of NavPress Publishing Group

ISBN 978-0-9982100-4-9

Cover design by Antonio Palmer

Library of Congress Control Number: 2017904573

This book is dedicated to the memory of my son, Deon. You were the shining light that made me smile the moment I saw you. Your joy for life gave all those around you joy. Until we meet again in heaven. I love you.

I also dedicate this book to my first true love, my other son Randy – my fighter, my protector, my strength! When you entered this world, I knew you would cause a disruption wherever you went. Allow God to order your steps and speak those things that are not as if they already were. Your sense of humor and wit causes all those around you to embrace your world as you see it. Continue to let us in on who you are in God! I love you eternally.

> The most powerful
> relationship
> you will ever have
> is the relationship with
> yourself.
>
> Steve Mariboli
> Fearless Soul

Acknowledgements

I want to thank my king, Bishop Antonio Palmer, my Boo, my man, my gift from God, for being patient, kind, and loving to me. You are always pushing me into my destiny by encouraging me to be me. I love being in love with you!

There are several people who come to my mind who inspired me over the years, so if I forget you, please forgive me. Elder Julius Crawford, Mother LaRuth Harper, Mary Carpenter, Tracey Cherry, Elder Terry Henson, Pastor Sheryl Menendez, Bishop Donald and Pastor Becky Fulton, Apostle Larry Lee Thomas, Bishop Craig Coates, and Pastors Frank and Stephanie Holloman. Also, I'd like to thank my armor bearers for life, Minister Charlene Hawkins and Jamie Massey. In addition, I thank God for the Intercessors of KCC, our Calvary Alliance church family, our covering, Bishop Courtney McBath and Lady Janeen, Pastor Jimmie Thomas and the KCC leadership team. I cannot forget my awesome parents, Samuel and Debbie Simms for guiding me in life, and the daughter I never had until my son married you, Kimberly – I want you to know that you never have to fight for my heart, it always belongs to you. You are the special jewel that has not been unearthed and I pray that when God removes the debris and allows that diamond to shine, your Mom-Mom will be right there cheering you on. To my "tried in the fire" son, Randy, you were predestined before the foundation of the world to bring forth the word of the Lord and that's why the enemy fights you so much. Guess what, Randy? Momma loves you unconditionally and I'm proud of the man that you are and the man that you are becoming. I want to shout out a very, very special thank you to Kingdom Celebration Center for loving me.

I honor my grandmother, Nanny, who is no longer here on Earth with us and my aunt, Baby, who treated me as her own daughter. I often tell my mother that I think she switched me at birth! Minister Terry Henson for packing up my home when my son died and taking care of my personal belongings, Pastor Rebecca Fulton for coming into my life during a time when I needed a true friend. You saw ME and loved me anyway. To Pastor Stephanie Holloman for being my ride or die!

Finally thank you Adonai for trusting your hardheaded and stubborn child with writing her story. You by far are the greatest Daddy I could ever ask for. I love you with such great passion!

Table of Contents

Introduction 1
Chapter One - Barbara 7
Chapter Two - Pregnant at 16 11
Chapter Three - Meeting God 15
Chapter Four - Marriage Gone Wrong 19
Chapter Five - Marriage Gone Right 27
Chapter Six - Death 39
Chapter Seven - The One Who Brought Me Life 57
Chapter Eight - Ministry 63
Chapter Nine - Business Naysayers 67
Chapter Ten - I'm Grateful for it All 73
Conclusion 77

About the Author

Introduction

Writing a book was never my ambition. For those who know my Choleric temperament, it was very hard for me to sit down and write for hours (even years). Writing a book takes so much time. You know it has to be a God-thing for me to be still enough to get this book done. If you know me, you know I'd rather speak into a recorder and then have someone else do the writing.

This book has been over twenty years in the making. It has been spoken over my life for more than thirty years that one day I would write a book (actually several books). Every time I hear someone say that to me in a prayer line, I would internally laugh and say, "Well, everyone is writing books these days, so Jesus, just let me live for you." I don't need a book to do that, but I guess there must be something about my life that He wants me to share and that He feels will help someone else's life.

In this book you will find that I had to learn to love myself the way God loves me. I had to learn during this life-journey to not feel as though I had to give my body to a man to feel my worth (thanks Honey for teaching me I'm worth the wait). I had to learn not to sell my body, mind, or emotions for security. I had to learn that parenting is more than pushing a baby out and that it takes a lifetime to raise your children. I had to learn that some people sitting in church can be very cruel, unforgiving manipulators, who can also be self-righteous, legalistic, and intolerant of people. I was one of those people. I had to learn that the world does not revolve around me and that just because I shed some tears does not give me the right to control the situation (ouch y'all).

Good lessons can cause you to change from that old nature to the nature of Christ. It teaches you to walk in the Spirit so that you will not fulfill the desires of this Old Flesh! (the Bible teaches us that).

I had to learn that it's okay to fail sometimes; it's okay that if you were faced with bad credit, you restore it. Life isn't over because you filed bankruptcy - you can recover and move on. And guess what else? I even learned that when people don't forgive me, it's okay because I serve a God who forgives and has cast my sins away as far as the east is from the west.

I must make you aware in this introduction that I'm not your typical First Lady, Sister, Pastor, or friend girl. When the Lord called me out of darkness, He called me out to have a voice and to not be silent. The enemy's number one priority against me is to try and keep me silent, especially my story. So, I've learned to be okay with myself, even if anyone else is not. And with this frame of mind, God has called me to write this book to inspire those who may need to get past the fear of the opinions of others.

Introduction

Please enjoy my experiences, as it has brought healing to my mind, will, and emotions. Don't be too disappointed if I don't quote any Scriptures in this book. I'd like to think that my life is an open book – like the old adage – my life is the sixty-seventh book of the Bible. Here, I'm simply opening it up for you to read.

I must honor the Lord, the Author and Finisher of my faith, for trusting me with my own story and I thank those – who I may or may not have named in this book – because you played a role in my story and the outcome of my life.

I also wrote this book because I want my children and grandchildren and generations to come to know that although I suffered some things, I also came out of my sufferings victoriously. Do I still cry sometimes? Absolutely! Do I still need those close relationships that will help me cultivate and grow into the millionaire that God has ordained for me to become? Yes!

One thing I do understand is that no matter how gifted, talented, or anointed I may be, it is all because His banner over me is love. He waves that banner over me with His grace, favor and forgiveness. That is what I will always keep before me.

As you read my story I pray that God will allow you to see that if He can bring me out of the darkest and most severe situations, He also can bring you out of yours.

> "Is anyone crying for help? God is listening, ready to rescue you. If your heart is broken, you'll find God right there; if you're kicked in the gut, he'll help you catch your breath. Disciples so often get into trouble; still, God is there every time." (Psalm 34:17-19)

We don't have any excuse to stay in the state that we are in. So get up, get a glass of water (as my friend, Martha, would say), and grab a blanket (as my friend, Steph, would say), or just hold the baby and read (as my daughter, Kim, would say). Whatever you do, don't make an excuse for not reading (Mrs. Char)! Don't run from the challenge (Jamice) – just do what the Master has called you to do (Natalie and Zenda) and watch how blessed and prosperous you will be! (These are names of some of the women in my church who I have had the privilege to mentor and counsel and whom I love dearly).

I am a woman with a story and with a past. I'm a woman who has been bruised and wounded but now healed from those very wounds and has moved forward in life. I am a woman who's been incarcerated and has a record, but now I am an entrepreneur with several honest and meaningful businesses. I am a woman who suffered loss and death of loved ones, but has received unspeakable strength from God. I am a woman who has been divorced and now remarried to the man of my dreams. Though I've experienced these

Introduction

tragedies and more in my life they led me to my greatest discovery – the grace of God. We all will go through some type of tragedy, suffer loss or will all experience difficulty. However, I have learned that it is not what you go through; it is how you go through it. My prayer is for you to gain a better understanding of God's strength that is made available for you through every tragedy you may face in your life. I will share with you my struggles but I will also share with you my strength. Thus, my story begins.

Chapter One

Barbara

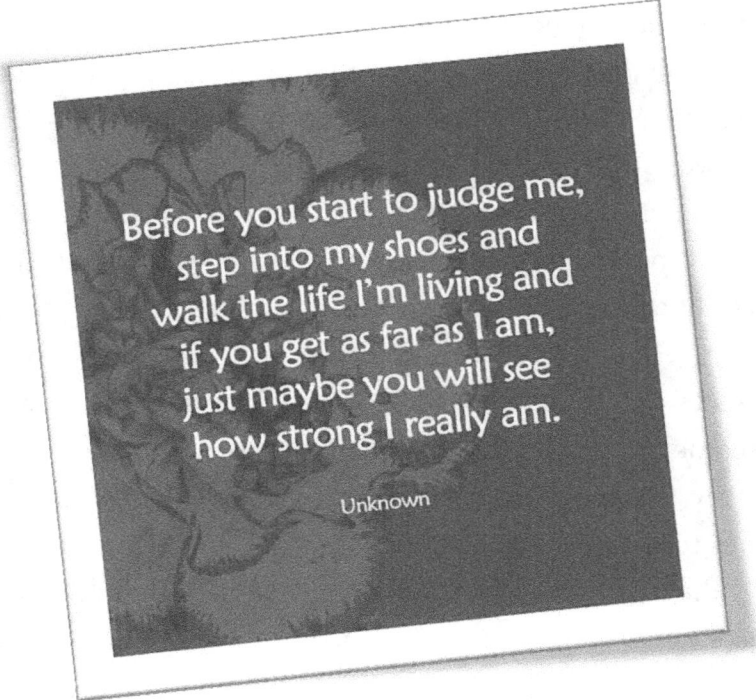

So what's really in a name? Who is Barbara? During a women's Bible Study, a great friend once told me exactly what my name meant. From that day forward things seemed to make perfect sense to me.

No Regrets

> The name *Barbara* means "stranger, foreigner, or one who is passing through."

When I was a child living on my grandparents' farm, my grandfather would often call me, "Doll." It made me feel special, unique, and loved. Although I was extremely shy and did not feel pretty, knowing that my grandfather viewed me that way always provided me comfort.

My name is a reflection of who I am and how God created me. Even though my parents named me, it was God who had already chosen my name before He created the foundation of the world. When He had me in mind, He knew who my parents would be and what I would have to endure to become the woman that He created in His own image.

My mother often talks about the way she grew up in a small town and wanting to explore "the city" as she so called it. She was always very vocal when I became an adult to share with me her experiences of abuse when she was married to my biological father. One thing she shared with me that still sticks out is one incident she had with my father. She remembers when I was conceived, but she also remembers the day he kicked her so hard in her stomach because he did not want her to have me. I could have been a miscarriage or she could have died. Do you know what that tells me? God must have truly had His hand on my life even while I was in my mother's womb, insomuch that the enemy never wanted me to make it to my destination, of being

Chapter One - Barbara

born. She shared with me that even after she gave birth to me, she was not allowed to hold me for seven days because I was sick. At a time when a mother and her daughter should be bonding, that moment was taken away from us. Although my mother and I have a relationship today, I know that there have been repercussions from that time until now.

Barbara (stranger, foreigner, someone passing through) speaks loudly in my mind as I recall my childhood, my teen years, and now my adulthood. I was never meant to fit in. I was never meant to walk with everyone. I know now why I feel like a stranger even around my friends and family. I know that my ultimate goal on Earth is to never look to the left or right, but always look forward to the One who is standing in front of me – my king, Jesus. My aim is always to get to Him!

As I reflect back over my life, I guess the earliest memory I have is of a five year old little girl holding her mother's hand and being escorted into my kindergarten class. I remember it being a bright, sunny day and just being happy that I was with my mother. I had no idea that she was about to leave me in a strange place. When the doors opened and the teacher said for me to come in because she was expecting me, fear gripped my mind. Who is she? What does she want? It was very overwhelming for a five year old to understand, especially a five year old who is extremely shy and introverted. I remember my mother walking away and me crying like crazy for her not to leave me. The teacher tried to comfort me but I was terrified. Maybe if my mother had explained the process and stayed with me for a while, I would have understood it better and not have been so terrified of the process. But she did not do that. That is why when my grandson headed to kindergarten, not only did his parents make it fun and exciting, but I was standing right there explaining to him that it was okay and that we would be waiting for him after school. These moments shape our entire life as it relates to how we will feel about ourselves and those around us. We really do become a product of our environment.

Needless to say, my kindergarten experience was the first of so many experiences that taught me to withdraw, hold in my feelings and not communicate. The enemy has a way of turning something as simple as going to school for the first time into a traumatic experience that affected me for years to come. But thank God that He knew me by name and decided at the right time to reveal to me what my name means. I'm just someone passing through this life representing a great King whose kingdom I have citizenship in. So now that kindergarten experience along with the other traumatic ones takes on new meaning; a meaning that shows me how I am to help others gain victory and strength over their life traumas.

Chapter Two
Pregnant at 16

Often people who criticize your life are usually the same people that don't know the price you paid to get where you are today.

    I came from a very small family. It was only me, my mom, my dad and my brother. Being the oldest, I guess you could say I was spoiled. My brother and I have always been like Night and Day. He would always say to me that my mother loved me more than he. I never thought that to be a true statement, because it seemed to me that whatever she gave me, she also gave to him. We did not come from a family of money, but my grandfather owned a farm and that is where I spent most of my time. He raised pigs, horses, chickens, dogs, and cats; you name it, he had it. We had apple trees, pear trees, blackberry bushes, raspberry trees, and fresh fruits and veggies. We even ate our own farmed eggs from our chickens. For water, we had a well in the backyard. However, we didn't have a shower in the house. Since we did not have running water in the house, my mom would have to heat some water on the stove and then pour it into the bathtub for us to take a bath. I can still see all the fun we had at family reunions at my grandparents' house. Unfortunately, I can also remember that it was during that time that I was molested at the age of eight years old. Since I was so shy it was easy for people to ignore me and it was easy for me to go off to a room or corner by myself where I was not missed. It was while I was in a room by myself that a family member came in and molested me.

    When I was in middle school my mother moved us to "the city" as she called it and this little country girl, who knew nothing about life, was about to become exposed to a new way of living. By the summer of my tenth grade year (going into my eleventh grade year) I met a young man. He said that he wanted me and I believed him to the point that I allowed him to have sex with me. And the first time I had sex, I got pregnant! Needless to say, I was pregnant at

Chapter Two - Pregnant at 16

sixteen, while going into my last year of high school. My mother had remarried by then and my stepfather was very instrumental in making sure that I finished school and did what I needed to do. He did not want me to use having a baby as an excuse. Can you imagine...I had to come home from school, do my homework and not go out on the weekends? I am so glad they helped me to keep my sanity. They were very instrumental in making sure that my newborn son was cared for and that he had what he needed. By the time he was three years old, I ended up giving my parents custody of him so that he could have health insurance, live in a nice home in a nice neighborhood and have a stable life. Most people think it makes you less of a mother when you give your child up for adoption, but for me it made me a better mother because I was smart enough to understand that if I were to raise him we would have lived in the projects and my son would have probably ended up a statistic. He always knew I was his mother and I saw him whenever I wanted to.

It was very difficult being sixteen with a baby and the father not being active in your child's life. It teaches you to grow up quickly (and that I did). What it didn't teach me was how to be a parent. Parenting is something that I was not ready for at the time. I didn't want to drop my baby off with any and everybody. I didn't want my child to end up molested like I was. But it was tough because, at that age, I still wanted to hang out with friends. Nevertheless, I wanted my child to have the best and the best for him was to live with my parents. What's even more fascinating is that when he was seventeen, I asked him if he was angry at me for giving him up for adoption. His response was, "Ma, I saw you all the time…I'm okay."

Chapter Three
Meeting God

My encounter with God was one of the most amazing things that ever happened in my life. In 1985, I went to a church service that was held in Washington DC and although I had been raised in the Methodist faith, I had never experienced anything like what I saw that night. As I entered the building of this storefront church, I saw people singing with great might and praising God like they knew He was right there watching them. Then the preacher got up to speak. He preached with such power and conviction. Once he was finished with his sermon, he asked if anyone wanted to be filled with the Holy Ghost. I sat in my seat watching as people began to speak in what I now know as "diverse kinds of tongues," which were their heavenly language. I found myself rocking back and forth in my seat and before I realized it I was at the front of the church standing in front of the pastor, crying uncontrollably! He asked me if I had accepted Jesus as my personal Savior and I confessed, "No." He then proceeded to lead me to Christ. I was still crying and screaming when he asked what I wanted God to do for me. I replied that I wanted what everyone else in the church had. I didn't know at the time what it was so I pointed to people speaking in tongues. He began to pray for me and the mothers of the church came around me and began to repeat the name, "Jesus, Jesus, Jesus..." all around me. Somehow, I fell to the floor and began to scream. I did not get filled with the Holy Ghost that night, but I must have been on the floor for like an hour. After the service I was so exhausted, but the pastor assured me that God wanted to fill me and that if I kept asking him, He would.

    I began my journey of seeking God through His word and learning how to pray and call upon His name. One morning while I was at home in my bathroom praying, I suddenly

Chapter Three - Meeting God

heard footsteps behind me. Although I was afraid, I also felt a sense of peace (if that makes sense). I began to cry. While I was crying, I heard in my head the tongues that everyone was praying in the church. Then I felt this hand touch my mouth and my back and I immediately began speaking in tongues in my bathroom! I was crying, speaking, shouting all at the same time. I had a true encounter with God. I was not filled in a traditional sense of being in the church and "tarrying" for His presence. He had a different plan for me as far as filling me with His Spirit.

 I went to church the following week for a nightly prayer service. Now in the past, when I came to an evening prayer service everyone would be praying out loud simultaneously and you could hear them. But I would go kneel in the back of the church somewhere and whisper my prayers to God. However, on this particular night as the people began to praise God, I began to raise my hands, lift my voice and blessed God. Before I knew it I was speaking in tongues again. Everyone began to look at me, and then everyone began to shout. It was pandemonium. They were all under the assumption that I received the Holy Spirit that night. What they did not know was that I received the Holy Spirit at home in my bathroom. God did a great work in me. I felt an overwhelming presence come upon me that I could never explain. He became my Source, my Refuge, my Strength and my Helper at that very moment. I understood who He was to me. He was to me the Most High God!

I met God in my bathroom that day. It was an experience that no preacher gave to me nor a mother at the church gave to me, and definitely I couldn't give it to myself. He wanted me to know for myself who He truly was and I'm thankful for the gift of the Holy Spirit.

From that time until now, I have not forgotten what my God has done for me. I serve Him not because I have to but because I want to. I have gone through lots of things in my life sometimes even questioning my relationship with Him. But I have concluded that nothing can separate me from the fact that He is my God.

Chapter Four
Marriage Gone Wrong

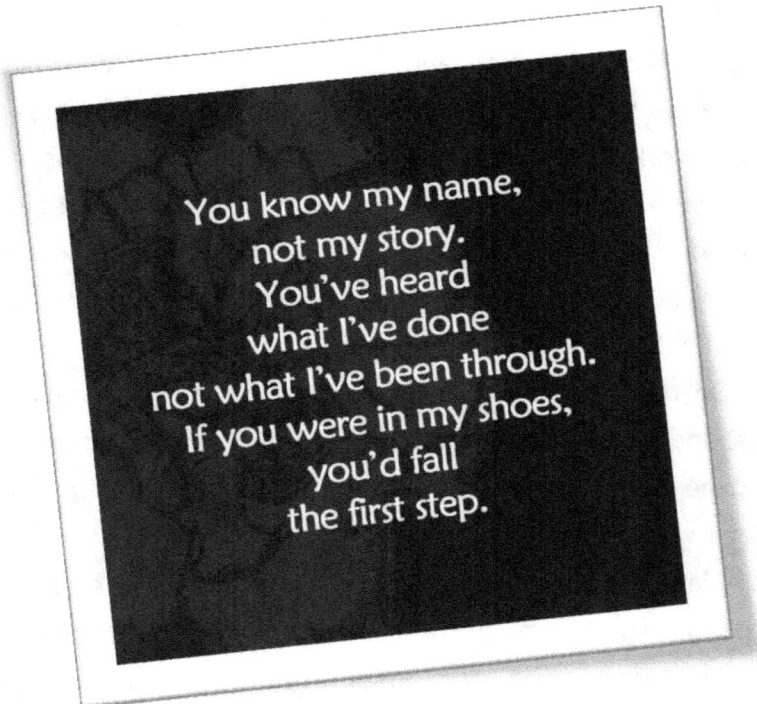

You know my name,
not my story.
You've heard
what I've done
not what I've been through.
If you were in my shoes,
you'd fall
the first step.

When you desire something bad enough, you normally get what you want. You know how, ladies, when we want a new pair of shoes but can't afford them, we will make a way to get them somehow. Well, it is safe to say that many of us are the same way when it comes to relationships, especially unhealthy ones. We overlook the little things to get what we want. We overlook stuff like, he wants to know where I am because he cares, or he doesn't want me to work because he wants to take care of me. Now don't get me wrong, this does not apply to every man, but it does in this case.

When I got married the first time, of course, my intentions were not to end up as a divorcee. My heart's desire, so I thought, was to make it last for a lifetime. It didn't work out for me that way at all because there was a lot of physical and verbal abuse. In the beginning I stayed because I loved him and we could work it out, then I stayed because "church" folks told me it was the right thing to do, until finally I got the courage to leave.

On the day that I left that abusive relationship, my ex-husband had locked me in the basement and informed me that he was taking our son, Randy Jr., with him to work and that I was to stay in the basement until he got back three days later! I guess because I looked so sad, he decided to allow our son to stay in the basement with me that night. I was thinking that he was coming back in the morning as he always did and take our son either to the sitter or along with him. When I got up that morning, the basement door was unlocked and he was gone. I felt as though that was the opportunity for me to call my mother. So I hurried to call her and told her to come get me. I left with only the clothes that I had on my back. That's right, I didn't pack a bag. I didn't

Chapter Four - Marriage Gone Wrong - from the Beginning

even take any bottles, pampers, or even baby wipes. I took my life and ran!

As I was going to my parents' house I could feel all the pain I had suffered; the abuse, the shame, the denial, the laughs of people, and the embarrassment of a failed marriage. I heard all kinds of words in my head so I didn't need anyone else to yell these things out to me. I heard words like, "Girl, I would have left a long time ago, you are so stupid, church or no church, I would have been out." Guess what? It is easier said than done, especially if you felt like you wanted it to work and did not want to fail God. All I knew at that moment is that I could finally get some air and that I could finally see things clearly. It was not me that he wanted, but my body. It wasn't a family that he wanted, but the mere image of one. It wasn't God that he desired, but the title (he was an elder in the church!).

Everything that I thought and knew as real was now gone. All of my friends who attended our church, my mother in the Lord, my pastor and his wife, were all people that I met when I came to church – which was the church my ex-husband introduced me to. It is the same church where I gave my heart to God. These were the people I knew I would never see again because I felt they had failed me. Don't get me wrong, I made plenty of mistakes. For example, every time they saw me, I had something negative to say about him not coming home, about the beating that I got, or the threats I received. I wanted them to be mad at him just like I was. I wanted someone to validate my pain. So every time I walked into a room, I told the world just how "bad" he was. I was reaching out for help but in the wrong way. The part that hurt me was that they began to lean toward his favor as though I was a "bad" wife. I'm sure they may have felt that way because of the way I verbalized my dislike of him. Whatever the case, I'm so glad I was able to leave that abusive marriage.

Since I could not find validation from the people I thought loved me and cared for me the most, I found it in "the world" via a man. Now, don't get me wrong, it did not happen overnight, but when you are lonely, unloved, broken, and misunderstood, the enemy has a way of sending the right person into your life to say, "Why do you look so sad, you are beautiful." You will reject it a few times, but sooner or later, you will begin to open your heart to the fact that someone noticed your pain and appears to want to heal it. I justified my meeting another man because my "husband" wasn't the man he pretended to be. I kept making so many excuses to try and see another man that when people in church saw me coming they went the other way.

I finally confessed to my pastor and his wife. They held me tight and consoled my pain. But afterward, whenever I would be at church, I felt as if everyone in the room knew my personal business. I wasn't too hurt by the fact of my pastor and his wife neglecting the confidentiality of my "junk." I was more hurt because people were saying that the Holy

Chapter Four - Marriage Gone Wrong - from the Beginning

Spirit revealed it, then acting so shocked and appalled that I would do such a thing. That just made me worse, because they acted as though they couldn't forgive me of my sin, yet they justified his!

What I'm about to say to you may make you cringe. God told me that I got what I asked for. You see, He never told me to marry him. Even my pastor had told me he was not going to perform the wedding because God didn't tell him we were supposed to be together. I ignored it all for what my flesh craved for. At that age, I thought that I was in love with him but what I really was looking for was security, finances, and a way to escape home. I learned some tough but valuable life lessons during my time with him. The only good thing that I gained from that relationship was my son.

Because I care deeply about my son, I cannot and will never go into too much detail, here or anywhere else, about everything that I endured and suffered at the hand of his biological father. I care that much for him and his stability. Thank God for making a way of escape for me. I will share this limited amount about the abuse that took place.

One of our first altercations took place one night after church. I had shared with my then husband that I wanted to get a job and that I had filled out an application to work at a bank. He told me, "No." So I went to my pastor and his wife to discuss it and asked if they could sit in as I shared with my husband how I did not want to sit in the house at 20 years of age and not work or not go to college. They said they would agree to sit with us but that whatever decision was made had to be between me and my former husband. After the meeting was over, we went home and it was the first time I experience verbal abuse from him. It scared me and I cried, once he saw the tears he backed off and later that week brought me flowers and took me out to make up for his "outburst."

Wherever I go, I always tell ladies that I don't put all the blame on him, but I take ownership of some of the things that I have done as well. I take responsibility for the part I played in the mixing of the scrambled eggs. I own up to the fact that I wanted a man to take care of me. At Eighteen or Nineteen years old, what did I really know about that? I was so naïve. My naiveté led to my demise. I own the fact that everyone around me was saying it was wrong, but I felt "grown" enough to make my own choices. Girlfriend was I wrong. Those choices were not good for me at all.

After I left the marriage, I moved back home with my parents. I remember going to bed at night waiting for everyone else to get to sleep so that I could get back up and go to a corner in the room to rock back and forth for fear that he would come and hurt me. I was losing my mind and most of all, I was losing my faith in God. That's how bad the abuse was. It had that kind of impact on my psyche. It was during this time that I walked away from my relationship with God because I began to feel that God had abandoned me. I had lost everything that I was familiar with. I no longer had a

Chapter Four - Marriage Gone Wrong - from the Beginning

home, a church family, my so-called friends, and what you would call a marriage.

Chapter Five
Marriage Gone Right

Happiness began for me the day I walked down the aisle with my new husband and said "I do." It was beyond my wildest dreams. I now have a wonderful husband and an excellent stepfather for my children. Whatever I desired of the Lord he granted it unto me. I didn't feel like I deserved this kind of happiness especially after a failed marriage and I surely didn't know how to enjoy it all. Sometimes you can get so used to being miserable that when God blesses you, you are always looking around the corner for the big bombshell to fall or for the floor to collapse from under you.

Having been previously in a verbal, emotional and physically abusive marriage, it was hard for me to fully receive the new man in my life. Beforehand, my life had been in such turmoil and disarray. I had a child at sixteen, left him in the care of my parents so that I could go off and experience life, then met a man who I thought was in love with me but ended up abusing me, and being damaged by the people and church he introduced me to. I was a wreck! I gave my life to Christ only to have the church abuse me by controlling my every thought and action. When I met my new man, I was now a mom of two children, going to college and was trying to find a career. What a blur my life was then. It's a blur because I just wanted to forget my past and press toward my future. The Lord had to teach me how to love again and how to open up my heart to someone else. And he used a great man of God, someone who was special to Him as well, to do this – the man of my dreams – my present husband. I know I took him through the ringer but he loved me through my process.

Now, after several years of growing pains, I can say that one of the things that I thank God for is giving me a second chance and teaching me how to love my husband the right

Chapter Five - Marriage Gone Right

way in spite of my past marital catastrophe. I enjoy waking up to him each morning and watching him get dressed. I like his swag and his daily task of taking care of himself. I love the way he looks, the way he smells, his style, and most of all, I love the way he loves God. I don't have a sure key to our success. All I can say is that as long as we both keep our eyes on Jesus and yield to Him, we remain successful as a couple. I can tell you in those rare moments that we mess up, I know it's because we both have lost our focus with God and need to get that back first before we can get it right with each other.

I was at bible study one night and one of the women in our church who is going to school to get her degree, started asking all the married women questions about their relationship. When she got to me with her question, she asked, "What is the one key that you could give me to write in my paper about successful marriage?" My answer was to understand the fact that I did not have to win every battle. That is what I learned early in my marriage.

When my husband and I first got married, it was difficult because he came from a background of always being taken care of by his mother, sister, women, and then the system. I came from a background of where you had to take care of yourself. Whether it was school, work, or family, you did what you needed to do to survive and move on. Can you imagine what it was like for us once we said, "I do." Just picture this man who is used to having his way and this woman who is independent and thinking to herself, "Please" get a grip!

I met my husband in a very unique way. We always say it was God ordained, but brace yourself when I tell you how we met. I was serving a four month sentence at a halfway house for committing a crime! One evening I was on my way to work (they allowed me to keep my job and serve my sentence) and while I was checking out to go to work, all the women at the facility were talking about this handsome guy who just showed up at the desk to check in. I really did not pay too much attention to what they were saying until I got to the desk to check out and he was there checking in. I noticed him at that moment and my heart melted. I had no idea why, but he made me very nervous. I did not know at the time that when he saw me he felt an immediate connection as well. Needless to say, I did not introduce myself. I signed out to go to work and went on my way. As the week went on, several of the people at the halfway house began to talk about the fact that this handsome guy was going to start a bible study group. Then the women all placed a bet of seeing who could get his attention first. Even though I was in a state of being angry with God, I still decided to attend one of the bible study sessions but for the wrong reason. I only attended to see what all the hype was about this cutie that I saw!

Once I went to his bible study session, I then realized that he was very serious about his faith and walk with God. But

Chapter Five - Marriage Gone Right

hey, I was up for the challenge. I began to talk to him about my life, my church family that had failed me, and my failed marriage at a very young age. I shared with him that I had a son when I was sixteen and that I had another son by my husband who I have now divorced. I laid everything on the table. I told him things I had never told anyone else in my life. I shared my molestation as a child, my insecurities as a girl, my instability to truly love, and how I felt like a failure for where I was today. He listened without judgment and prayed with me on several occasions. But ladies, keep in mind, I was very attracted to him and I could sense that he was attracted to me as well.

Since I worked the midnight shift for my job, it was easy for him to call the call center and talk to me at night for free. He told me about his life and how he ended up incarcerated for four years. He shared with me how that he came from a good home, that he was a military brat (both his mother and father served, including his sister and brother). He had even served in the military for three years and had planned to go to college after receiving the GI Bill. However, when he got home, he tried to make some fast money the easy way and it cost him four years of his life. It was his first time ever being in trouble. He shared how he felt like he let down his parents and family. He gave his life to Christ while experiencing his lowest point in prison.

So, there we were growing closer and closer each day. One day, as I was sharing with him how angry I was at my ex-husband for the way he treated me and how he allowed other people in the church to tell him how to treat me, this cute, man of faith lets me get it all out, then he looks at me and says, "In order for you to move on, you will have to forgive your ex-husband."

> "Eyes have not seen, ears have not heard, neither has it entered the heart, the things that God has in store for those that love him."
> (1 Corinthians 2:9)

Let me digress back to the moment I got to the Halfway House. The day I pulled up on the parking lot of the Halfway House I was petrified. I had no idea what to expect or what would happen to me there. I had never committed a crime and had never even had a speeding ticket. So here I am, this little naïve church girl headed to a minimum security prison of sorts.

As I mentioned earlier, I was allowed to go to work while I was there so that I could pay back my restitution for what I had stolen. I worked the midnight shift at the airlines so I was on my way to the front desk to sign out as the women in my room were yelling, "Girls, look at this fine piece that is checking in." One of them stated, "Don't touch him, he is mine" (trust me she meant it too). I saw him from a distance but paid no attention because that was not my interest. I didn't have marriage on my mind, let alone, being in another

Chapter Five - Marriage Gone Right

relationship. My focus was to do whatever I had to do to get out of the hellhole I was in. Besides, I had already been there for two months and was counting down the next two months to go by as fast as the last two had.

But then I walked to the front desk and while as I was checking out, he was checking in. Now some of you may think I'm crazy but as I walked by him I knew at that moment that we would be together. Our eyes met and we said hello and out the door I went. When I came back from work the next morning all the ladies were talking about him and betting on who would get him first (if you know what I mean). As the weeks went on, he began to be known as the "preacher" at the facility and they allowed him to hold bible study once per week. As I mentioned before, I jump on the band wagon with all the other girls and decided to go just to "see "him. Little did I know that God had another plan for me.

As the cute preacher began to talk about the word of God, his title was on "Forgiveness." It rang a bell because I was still very bitter after I left my marriage. After the bible study I began to hang around and talk to him about what I was going through and how I felt God had abandoned me. He took me to the Word and told me I had to forgive everyone including myself, and then he prayed for me. In my mind, my thought pattern was "man don't you know I want you, I just told you I was a backslider and that I was angry at

God and the world." All I wanted to do was sin at that moment! (LOL)

He began to share his story with me about how he ended up here and how he had been in prison for four years and was not about to allow any woman, especially at a halfway house, to cause him to mess up what he had given God for four years. As stories go, we spent time sharing the Word, he helped me find my way back to God and we developed a friendship that I cherish to this day.

One night I had a dream and I shared it with him. I told him how God had spoken to me about us and that I saw us getting married. His response was that God had not shown that to him and that he was not making any decision unless God speaks to him as the man first. I was devastated, but God was teaching me even in that moment that you must give up your control and manipulation in order to receive from me. You see, I'm not saying that God did not give me the dream, but what I am saying is that He never told me to share it.

When it was close to the time for him to leave, I began to ask him what his plan was. Was he going back to Virginia or staying in Maryland and he told me whatever God wanted was what he would do. One day on my way out for work, he handed me a dollar bill with some words written on it in Spanish. When I got to work I asked my friend, who is Hispanic, to tell me what it said. The words were something like, "*Yo quiero te mucho.*" She said matter of fact, it says, "I *love you much."* Once she said those words I cried because I knew then that he felt the same way about me that I felt about him.

The next week we went to the park for another picnic and it was then that he asked me to marry him. He shared with me at that time that he also had a dream and as we compared them, he had the exact same dream that I had.

We married months later and have been together ever since. One of the many things I love about my husband is that he taught me that I did not have to give him my body in order to know that he loved me. He loved me for who I am and showed me and still shows me every day.

I'm thankful for those trials, I'm thankful for prison, I'm thankful for pain, because it led me to freedom!

Sometimes ladies we really don't deserve all the good that we have. If God were to pull back the scales so that people could really see our mess, we would be so ashamed. It was during my most depressed, ashamed, humbling and worst time of my life that God sent my Boaz – the man of my dreams into my life. People always ask how my husband and I met and when I tell them, they are amazed. Guess what? I'm amazed myself at what God did for me and I now know that "All things work together for the good of them that love God and are the called according to His purpose" (Romans 8:28).

You are probably wondering how I ended up at that halfway house anyway. You probably want to know what crime I committed. Well, while married to my first husband I was seeking out a way to leave him, but I did not have access to bank accounts or money, but my job did. I decided that the only way out was to take some money and I told myself that "I would put it back" over time. I was in a trusted positon at a very high level job in Washington D.C. and they never audited anything I did based upon who I was.

Well one day that same ex-husband went to my employer and told them I was on drugs, etc. (all of which was not true) so that I would lose my job. When he did that it actually sparked an investigation and an audit of everything I did on my job, which led to me being charged with a crime. That's how I got caught and it led me to a four month sentence at the halfway house. But even God was gracious then. I only received four months when I should have gotten 40 years – that's another book all in itself. On top of that, the judge allowed me to go to work at night and report back to the halfway house during the day. The greatest part of all, this crime took me from my misery and led me to the man of my dreams. I was escorted from my misery by the mercy of God! The reason why I say it was His mercy is because even when I felt like giving up on Him, He looked beyond my weak, failing heart and saw my need. Like the apostle Paul said, "But God who is rich in mercy!" Meeting him was like a breath of fresh air. I could breathe again. He became a new friend who led me back to God. After all that I had gone through in my

Chapter Five - Marriage Gone Right

previous marriage I never would've thought to meet the man God handpicked for me.

Chapter Six
Death

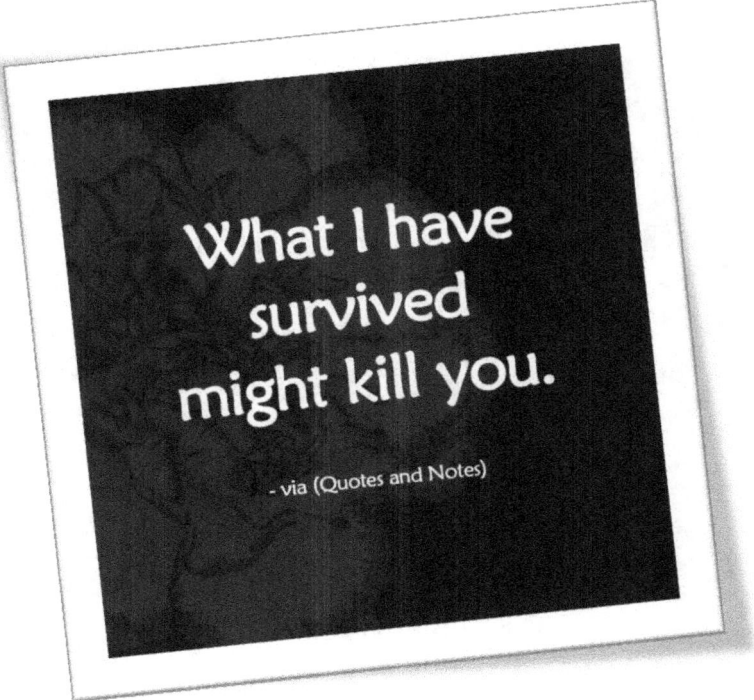

I hide in dark places
Disguised as brilliant light
I cast doubt upon the mind
Distinguishing the joy inside

No Regrets

I wait patiently for the moment
I prance upon the heart
I dance inside the mind
Distinguishing the joy inside

No need to fix my problem
No need to analyze
I cast doubt upon the mind
Distinguishing the joy inside

Who knew my grip would tighten
Who knew the pain would not subside
I dance upon the mind
Distinguishing the joy inside

When I deliver the final blow
No more worries you will find
The dancing upon the mind is gone
The joy inside erased the mind

Goodbye world and all its ill
Goodbye family
Goodbye

Suicide
Written by: Barbara Palmer

Chapter Six - Death

As I mentioned earlier in the introduction, when you have children you should always expect the unexpected. For example, they will sometimes fall and hurt their knees or lose their first tooth, maybe even run a high fever. You expect to wait up for them when they go out to drive your car for the first time. You expect to be a proud parent as they walk across the stage to graduate high school.

But one unexpected incident took place in my life that I'll never forget. I didn't expect to come home two days prior to the 9-11 World Trade Center attack and find my nineteen year old son, Deon, had taken his life. I didn't expect my whole world to be turned upside down in a matter of seconds. I didn't expect to feel such agonizing pain so great that even my tears could not express. I didn't expect that I could survive such a horrible event.

As a mother, as a pastor's wife, and as a professional who works in the Human Service field, you ask all the questions that could be asked and blame yourself for everything that went wrong:" You may ask yourself questions like, "Was I a good parent?" "What did I do to deserve this?" "Did I teach him great values?" "Where is my God in all this?" "What will my friends, church family, and peers think of me?" Then you realize that it was never about you, but about the hidden pain that our son was experiencing alone.

In the African American community, there was the stigma, the fear and misconceptions about suicide and depression. As a mother, I did not know that depression is a disease that can be treated. I did not know that you could get counseling and treatment for it. I did not know that you could find hope by seeking help. All I knew was that in our community, whether it was the church community or the African American community it brought shame to mention suicide.

Despair became my best friend because with suicide cases oftentimes there is no closure. And so it was with my son's death – no closure. I had to face the fact that I could not turn back the hands of time and "fix it." I could not will him to come back. Just like some of you who are reading this book today, no words could solidly comfort me. But one thing we share in common is the fact that we all decided to get up and face another day without our loved one. Sometimes during our days we may have sudden memories of them like a smile, a joke, a certain color, a birthday, a smell or even a favorite song.

I stand here today, many years later, finding solace when I remember my son, Deon, as this awesome, young man who made an impression on so many lives. He wanted to be a vet. He had a great love for animals. Oh how he loved his dogs! He also had such an overwhelming love for his family, especially his Granny and his brother Randy. He loved his friends and was respected and loved dearly by his friends in return. Still to this day, some of his friends visit his gravesite; a couple of them even have tattoos honoring him as a friend never forgotten. Moreover, hundreds of his friends and

Chapter Six - Death

fellow classmates attended his funeral finding themselves at the altar asking the Lord to come into their lives.

So, I've concluded that now it doesn't matter to me what people think in the church community or how the African American community responds when I share my story about my son's fall to suicide. What really matters now is that I share it as a testimony of how God has strengthened me in hopes that someone else will gain strength and know that someone cares and that they have support.

Suicide is no longer a "secret." It has no prejudice nor does it care about your economic status. We must begin as a nation to spread the word that depression is real and that you can receive help. We must talk about our fears about this taboo topic so that another family does not have to experience the same pain that I carry with me today. I thank God for His overflowing strength each day that enables me to endure the pain that I have had since 2001.

Every sixteen (16) minutes someone in the United States dies of suicide and every seventeen (17) minutes someone is left to make sense of it.

I am one of those persons who were left to try and make sense of it all. I was left to grieve. I never thought that my handsome, intelligent, prosperous, educated son would take his own life. What would spark a young man who was afraid to even swallow a pill to end up taking a gun to do such a hideous thing to himself?

No Regrets

All of my life I wanted my two children to have the best of everything. I wanted them to have a good education, grow to love the Lord and to treat others with respect and dignity. Yes, I was one of those "crazy" mothers who made sure she knew where her children were, how they were doing in school and the type of friends they were hanging around. It's funny how life is. My child did not smoke, drink, steal, or cheat. I thought to myself how could such a horrible thing happen to a good child? What was his crime but falling in love and not knowing what to do with a broken heart? Sadly, there are millions of teenagers all over the world, on a daily basis, contemplating suicide. This is one of the reasons why I wrote this book. I wrote it for that teen struggling with thoughts of taking their life because of depression, fear, loneliness or being heartbroken from a failed relationship. I wrote it for those mothers trying to raise a teen that seem to be in a dark place in their life, for those spouses whose marriage has gone wrong and for those fathers and friends who sit back and wonder what happened and why they couldn't save their friend and loved one.

I also wrote this book for myself because God said that it would also help me in my healing. During his pastoral counseling days, my husband would always encourage people about *bibliotherapy* – healing through reading. And the same holds true for writing. God knew that writing this book would bring added healing and therapy to my hurting soul. It had taken about eight years for me to be healed from

Chapter Six - Death

the grief. God would finally provide me with a level of peace that I had never known. His peace began to sustain my broken heart and my perplexed mind like never before. "And the peace of God which passed all understanding shall keep your hearts and minds through Christ Jesus" (Philippians 4:7).

In writing this chapter it could very well be the opportunity to share my son with the rest of the world and be the proud, doting Momma as I tell you about all he accomplished in such a short period of time. This is the chapter where I can now tell all of you that he is a successful Veterinarian, married, and has x amount of children. Oh, I can tell of his advanced career, how much money he makes, and what type of house he lives in. This could have been one of those happy ending stories that all parents expect to tell the world about their children. However, this chapter unfolds a different kind of story. It is that of a life that was just beginning to flourish but like a blade of grass it vanished in the wind. Unfortunately, it is a story of an abbreviated life which made an indelible mark on many other lives.

I can remember being in labor for eighteen long hours with Deon. This same baby that I finally got to bring home from the hospital became a child who was always afraid of any type of pain. I mentioned earlier that he did not like to swallow pills nor did he like to have blood drawn. This same baby who was afraid of the smallest level of pain grew up to be a handsome teenager, smart and educated, who loved baseball and animals. Oh, let me tell you about my firstborn!

No Regrets

I remember the day I came home from high school and my father was standing at the door. He said, "Don't even take your coat off because you are going with your mother to the doctors." "For what?" I replied. He answered, "To find out if you are pregnant." My heart was beating so fast I could hardly breathe. I can still remember the silence in the car as my mother drove me to the doctor's office. I can still remember the exam and the sound of the doctor's voice when he announced to my mom, "She is five months pregnant." Then she instructing me to stop wearing tight jeans because it could affect the baby. I recall her saying, "You are a high risk pregnancy." I had always wondered what that meant. I now realize that back then when you were sixteen years old and pregnant, it was automatically considered high risk because of my age. In the car going home my mother did not say a mumbling word to me. Once we got back to the house, I saw my father sitting on the couch when my mother opened the door. All she did was burst into tears and said to him, "She is five months pregnant."

It's funny how the day that Deon was born was just like any other day. I got up to get ready for school. (As a senior in high school I wanted to make sure I had collected everything I would need to be out to have this baby and return to school because I wanted to graduate on time). While I was getting out of bed that morning, I felt something warm running down my legs. My mother informed me that it

Chapter Six - Death

was my water breaking. So off to the doctor's office we went, and then to the hospital. As I stated before, I was in labor for over eighteen hours, trying to push him out, hoping that this was a dream that I would wake up from. After hours of pushing, the doctors decided that my pelvic bone was not large enough for the baby's head to come through, so I had to have an emergency C-section. I can see why – Deon was born on October 1, 1981 at 8:56 pm weighing 8lbs, 9ozs! My little, skinny 99 pound self was exhausted and afraid at the same time. I had so many questions and no answers. "What would I do with a baby? Who would watch him while I went to school? Would I have to drop out of school? And so on and so on.

I ended up coming home two days before he did from the hospital. The doctors had kept him at the hospital because he was jaundice. The morning he was released from the hospital, I remember staring out of the window as I watched his father and my mother bring him inside the house. He was so beautiful. I knew then that I would love him the rest of my life and do whatever I had to do to make sure he was happy and taken care of.

Since I was still considered a minor and under the care of my parents, all of my expenses became their expenses, including nightly feeding, diaper changes, and staying up late. As a sixteen year old, all I knew was that I wanted to finish school and that a crying baby was not helping. So what did my parents do? They changed their schedules around so that one of them would be home during the day with the baby just so I could finish school. I went to school every day and was home by noon. This was the schedule I needed in order to be an early graduate.

My parents decided to move into a new home and allowed me to stay in the apartment so that I could finish school and work. Eventually school, work and baby became too much for me. Since I knew my parents could care for my son far better than I could as a sixteen year old, I finally gave them legal custody. Now before you go off judging me and talking all kinds of stuff such as "I could never give my child up or why would you do that?" let me tell you why.

I was sixteen, going to school, no parenting skills, and no sense of responsibility when it comes to raising a child. I knew that I did not want to be on welfare all my life and I knew that I wanted a future so that I could take care of my son. When my parents adopted him, I could see him whenever I wanted to, he knew I was his mother, and he could visit me at any time.

Did it hurt me to have to call my parents to ask how he was doing or if I could come see him? YES! Did it hurt on holidays when they said it was not good to interrupt his family time? YES! But do I look back today and think I made the wrong choice? NO! My parents loved me enough to allow me to finish high school, go to college, and begin my life as an adult and I loved my son enough to know that I

Chapter Six - Death

could not provide the things for him to grow into the fine young man he was without them.

Deon eventually came back to live with us when he was a teenager and not because he was running away from my parents, but because it was now time. As I mentioned before, I would sometimes ask him if he ever resented me for not being there when he was younger. He would always say, "Ma, you know you my girl! I knew you loved me and that Granny and Pop-Pop helped you out. I thank you for that."

You would have to know and be acquainted with my parents in order to understand his comment. My father was chief of police and my mother worked for the same department. My father was a professor at Bowie State and believed strongly in education and equality for African American people, so Deon was in great hands. My mother, being who she is, would "dote" all over Deon as if he were here prized possession. You see, a few years before I got pregnant, she was pregnant and lost her baby. So for her, this was God's way of answering her prayers. She loved Deon in ways that she never loved me and I was grateful.

When Deon was in high school life took a dramatic turn for him because my father had died of lung cancer. I don't feel he fully recovered from losing the man who raised him and was his biggest supporter. They were inseparable. This was his first battle with depression, but it was very subtle.

He had a girlfriend (his one and only) who he loved and adored. I can recall when I wanted him to take a young lady from our church to the prom because she did not have a date and his reply to me was, "Mom, you are the one who taught me to be faithful. So how would that look if I took some other girl to the prom and I have a girlfriend?" I could not argue with that!

During the following summer after graduation his girlfriend broke up with him and it was so devastating to him to the point that he became very depressed and withdrawn. I saw it, but thought that he would "bounce back" from it all. Unfortunately, he never did. Now I must warn you, you will really think that what I'm about to say is really crazy but here goes....

I knew that something was going to happen to him. I could sense it. I would have dreams about it, but I just never knew what it was. I knew that I was going to lose him; insomuch that I even told him that the enemy was trying to take him out and we prayed together. No matter what we did or how we prayed, ultimately his decision was still his to make and ultimately he made his erring choice.

I could write an entire book about mental illness and the church; how mental illness is real, yet we in the church want to "cast" it out. I can't tell you how many people told me my son was in hell because he committed suicide. I even believed it myself. What lies we tell each other in the church to "comfort" our own flesh! We grow up in the church with such legalism and self-righteousness. We will be so shocked

Chapter Six - Death

and surprised when we get to heaven and see certain people and we will be like, "What are you doing here?"

He's gone and there is nothing I can do about it. Was I angry at the time? Yes! Here was the second time that I was mad at God! First with the abuse from my previous marriage and now my teenage son committed suicide. Yes, I wanted to leave the church especially with the stares of the self-righteous looking at me with eyes of condemnation. I even wanted to leave my husband because he had refused to commit me into a mental institution. I thought I was losing my mind. I stopped reading the Bible. I stopped praying. I didn't want to hear about God and I didn't want to hear His voice.

I couldn't seem to get a handle on my life until one day a dear bishop shared some kind words and sound advice to me that still ring true for me today. I shared with him that I felt so disconnected to God and that I did not want to talk, hear, or feel him. I asked him if that was wrong and his response was that it was okay because God was going to allow me to live off the residue of all the prayers I had prayed for other people and their children; so just live on the residue. It was the best advice anyone could give me as it helped me go from religion and maybe a form of godliness to a greater relationship with my heavenly Father. I began to become stronger in Christ as a result of that one powerful word from the man of God. Sometimes all it takes is one word from the Lord and it can be a healing balm for your sick soul.

I did not write this chapter for people to agree with me. I wrote this chapter for those who are grieving like I did and hoping that they can identify with my revelation. I sincerely believe that what the bishop said to me was for others too. It was for anyone who is experiencing a similar tragedy like I have. You, too, can live off of the residue of previous and present prayers sent up to God on your behalf. Let the word of the Lord set you free.

Below are some statistics about suicide:

> In 2005, suicide ranked as the third leading cause of death for young people (ages 15-19 and 15-24); only accidents and homicides occurred more frequently
>
> Every 2 hours and 11 minutes, a person under the age of 25 commits suicide.

Question: "What is the Christian view of suicide? What does the Bible say about suicide?"

Answer: According to the Bible, whether a person commits suicide is not what determines whether he or she gains entrance into heaven. If an unsaved person commits suicide, he or she has done nothing but "expedite" his or her journey to the lake of fire. However, the person who committed suicide will ultimately be in hell for rejecting

Chapter Six - Death

salvation through Christ, not because he or she committed suicide. The Bible mentions five specific people who committed suicide: Abimelech (Judges 9:54), Saul (1 Samuel 31:4), Saul's armor-bearer (1 Samuel 31:4-6), Ahithophel (2 Samuel 17:23), Zimri (1 Kings 16:18), and Judas (Matthew 27:5). All of them were wicked, evil, sinful men (not enough is said regarding Saul's armor-bearer to make a judgment as to his character). Some consider Samson an instance of suicide (Judges 16:26-31), but Samson's goal was to kill the Philistines, not himself. The Bible views suicide as equal to murder – that's what it is – self-murder. God is the One who is to decide when and how a person should die. To take that power into your own hands, according to the Bible, is blasphemy to God.

What does the Bible say about a Christian who commits suicide? I do not believe that a Christian who commits suicide will lose salvation and go to hell. The Bible teaches that from the moment a person truly believes in Christ, he or she is eternally secure (John 3:16). According to the Bible, Christians can know beyond any doubt that they possess eternal life no matter what happens. "These things I have written to you who believe in the name of the Son of God, that you may know that you have eternal life, and that you may continue to believe in the name of the Son of God" (1 John 5:13). Nothing can separate a Christian from God's love! "For I am persuaded that neither death nor life, nor angels nor principalities nor powers, nor things present nor things to come, nor height nor depth, nor any other created thing, shall be able to separate us from the love of God which is in Christ Jesus our Lord" (Romans 8:38-39). If no "created thing" can separate a Christian from God's love, and even a Christian who commits suicide is a "created thing," then not even suicide can separate him from God's love. Jesus died for all of our sins...and if a true Christian were to, in a time of spiritual attack and weakness, commit suicide – that would be a sin that Jesus died for.

This is not to say that suicide is not a serious sin against God. According to the Bible, suicide is murder; it is always wrong. I would have serious doubts about the genuineness of faith of anyone who claimed to be a Christian yet committed suicide. There is no circumstance that can justify someone, especially a Christian, taking his or her own life. Christians are called to live their lives for God – the decision on when to die is God's and God's alone. Perhaps a good way to illustrate suicide for a Christian would be from the Book of Esther. The Persians had a law that anyone who came before the king uninvited could be put to death unless the king extended his scepter towards the person - indicating mercy. Suicide for a Christian would be forcing your way into seeing the King instead of waiting for Him to summon you. He will point His scepter towards you, sparing your eternal life, but that does not mean He is happy with you. Although it is not describing suicide, the Bible verse 1 Corinthians 3:15 is probably a good description of what happens to a Christian who commits suicide: "He himself will be saved, but only as one escaping through the flames."[1]

---

[1] Recommended Resource: *Suicide: A Christian Response: Five Crucial Considerations for Choosing Life* by Gary Stewart.

Chapter Seven

The One Who Brought Me Life

Some church folks always expect pastors' kids to be angels. They place high expectations on them that they would never place on themselves or even their own children (now this could be a book all in itself). Some churches make it so difficult for the pastor's children and their family to make any mistakes or learn from them and grow. Our other son, Randy, is one of those children that the church has always placed high expectations on and he was one of those children who did not conform to what the church wanted.

You ever have a child that from the time they are in the womb you know that they must be called to a special purpose because of all the hell you are going through just trying to carry them? Well, our son Randy is that child. From the time I became pregnant I would get sick all the time. I would faint all the time and morning sickness was my way of life for those nine months. Right after he was born, he was taken back to the hospital because he had a fever for seven days that they could not break; he almost died. Then there was the time when he was about two or three years old that he decided to run out in the middle of the street in downtown Washington D.C. while traffic was coming in both directions. God truly gave His angels charge over him. Then there was the time that he opened a hard piece of candy at church and choked on it. Luckily, one of the members who were studying to be a nurse at the time came in the door as he was gasping for air and turning colors and extracted the hard candy. I have more stories concerning him like these that I could write for days.

Randy did not have a difficult home life, but his temperament, personality and self-will was enough to keep

Chapter Seven - The One Who Brought Me Life

me and his father on our feet. He was never understood as a child (and as an adult) - either you like him or you hate him. When he was 21 days old I took him to church because it was a custom at our church that when a child reaches 21 days old, God would release a special prophetic word concerning that child's life. The word over Randy's life was that he was called as a prophet and that he would speak to nations of things that would be hard to comprehend and believe. He was chosen to always protect me and that every spiritual gift that I have would be tripled within him.

I remember an incident that happened on his first day of school. While on the school bus going to kindergarten, the kids were all talking about Christmas and Santa Claus. Randy tells all the kids on the bus that there wasn't any Santa Claus and that their parents were the ones who were bringing all the gifts.

Then, while he was in the third grade, we decided to sign him up for karate classes to deal with his "energy" only for him to get on the school bus and walk up to a 5th grader who had been picking on him and hit him so hard that he broke the child's nose. So no more karate!

In the seventh grade he gets mad at a teacher and tells him that he would blow up the school if he said anything to him again. Of course everyone in the world was called in for that meeting. We moved him to a private Christian school in hope that it would help him but to no avail. He gets to the school and tells his new found friends who asked him what he was doing over the weekend that his parents were taking him to the movies. At this Christian school going to the movies was considered a no-no. One day Randy says to the teacher, "How are you going to say a movie is a sin when you were in the gym cursing today?" Well, I'm sure you can guess what happened to him after saying that to the teacher.

Randy was lost after his brother died. He wanted to numb his pain by doing things that were destructive so that he could stop feeling. I can't tell you how he survived the way he did the first year of his brother's death. He had to learn to be an only child, move from his school, leave his friends and go to another school and try and fit in, even stay with church folks while we looked for someone else to stay because I couldn't live in the same house that his brother died in. That was a lot for a 12 year old to experience. He created a character and became this person we did not know anymore. Randy would use drugs, stay out all night, disrespect us, and was always angry. Things were so bad that there were times the police were at our door asking questions. I would pray to God and say, "I've already lost one child, I can't take it if I lose another. Lord, please do what you need to do to save him, just don't kill him!

It had gotten so bad that his father and I decided that it was best to send him away to Job Corp so that he could get himself together since he wasn't interested in finishing school. We had signed all the necessary paperwork for him to be leaving on the following Monday. However, during the

Chapter Seven - The One Who Brought Me Life

same week that we signed all the papers, Eddie James Ministries, came to our church. Eddie's ministry deals specifically with troubled youth and young adults. I asked Randy to come to church with me. Of course, he never wanted to come to church and if he did he was high or carrying a gun and just sitting in church despondently. Fortunately, for whatever reason, that Sunday he did come to church. When Randy was about to leave Eddie stopped singing in the middle of a song and called him up. Keep in mind, Eddie did not know Randy or his situation. He had picked him out of a crowd of about 300 people. He told Randy that God wanted him and that this was the time for him to yield to God. And who could ever imagine that on that very night he would give his heart to the Lord. Not only that, but he packed his bags and went on the road with Eddie James. God answered my prayer! He knew that I could not bear losing another son.

Randy never had it easy because of the call of God that is on his life. He eventually ended up staying on the road with Eddie James Ministries for about three years which taught him how to pray and seek God's face for his ministry which also helped him to grow into his call. His voice carries a weight that is scary and almost intimidating to all who come in contact with him. Some think that because he is young he does not know what he is talking about but in reality he just has wisdom far beyond his years and he is a great student of the word of God. Sometimes just his walking into a room is enough to send people to walk in the other directions.

I want his gift to be used for the kingdom of God no matter how others view him because I know that in the end he is called and chosen by God for this season. He is a Millennial child who is not afraid to speak his truth whether people like it or not.

Chapter Eight
Ministry

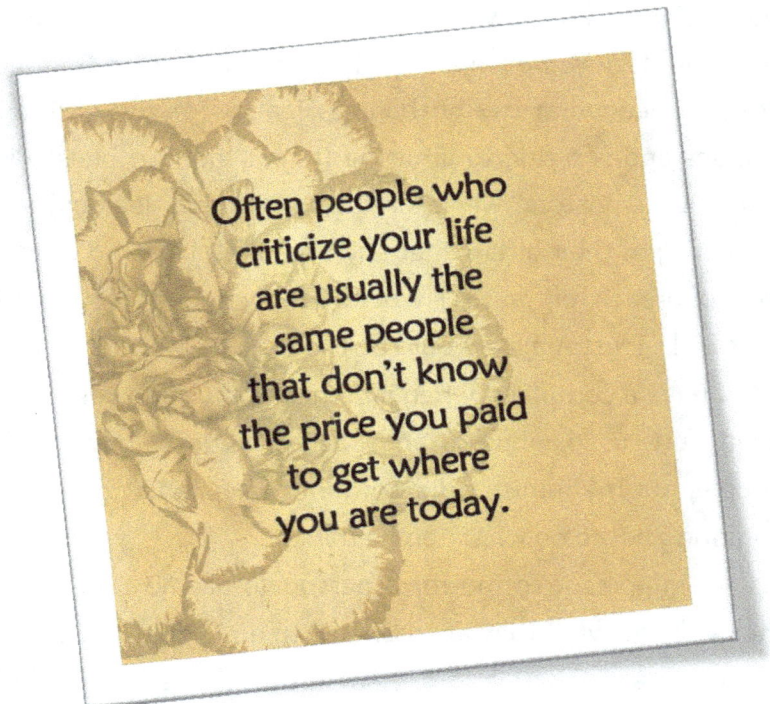

Often people who criticize your life are usually the same people that don't know the price you paid to get where you are today.

Everywhere my husband and I go other pastors' wives always ask me the same question, "Do you speak (preach)?" My answer is always the same, "I don't desire it." Mind you, this does not mean I can't, or that if God asked me to speak I would say no to Him. It simply means that I don't need to be behind a pulpit nor do I need to be called "Pastor, Prophet, Teacher, or Evangelist." I do not need a title to do what I have to do for Him. I don't say this arrogantly, but I know who I am in God and I know my role and I like to stay in my lane. I don't need to wear a red, purple, royal blue or black clergy shirt to let the world know I can preach. I just choose to serve. It does not make me less of a woman of God, nor does it mean that my husband is jealous of my gifts and abilities and is trying to limit me (I hear the horrible stories from other pastors' wives of their husband's jealousy and devaluing of their gifts). If at any time I felt like God wanted me to preach or teach I would simply mention it to my husband. Trust me, he would be the first to say, "Go for it." I don't have a complaint when it comes to my call. Yes, I have been hurt, used, abused, and pushed aside in ministry by people, but my ministry did not fade, disappear, nor lose its anointing based on what people think.

It's important to me for a person to always stay within their call and what they are assigned to do. Too many people try to imitate others and get outside of the realm in which God has called them. The calling of God on my life is to walk alongside my husband and to ensure that the vision that was given to him by God is followed out so that he can continue to hear from God for the furtherance of the kingdom of heaven on Earth.

I'm not bashing the church (because I love God's people), but some folks in ministry can be very funny-acting to me.

Chapter Eight - Ministry

Sometimes they love me and sometimes they don't. Most of the time they don't understand my role, nor my passion for what I do, but I'm okay with it. During our earlier years of pastoring it used to disturb me but the Lord has grown me in this area. Now, I just smile and pray for them (okay, sometimes I've gotta shake my head – SMH). I've learned to live peaceably with all men if it be possible.

When my husband and I started our first church back in 1995 I never imagined how hard it would be or how cruel people can be. To me, church folks can be on the top of the very-cruel-people list, because they hold you to a standard that they themselves can't live up to. If everything is right in their world, they love you; if everything is wrong in their world, it somehow becomes the pastor or the pastor's wife's fault.

At this point in life, I enjoy ministry because I now realize that 'people are just people' and some of them are in your life for a reason and some for a season. Some people will love you and some people will leave you. As I think back over my walk and growth from a young pastor's wife with no training to a seasoned pastor's wife, I would say that I'm very thankful to God for my journey. And He didn't speed up the process or shorten it for my sake. He has taught me so much about myself in 20 years of ministry. It was definitely an "On the job training" experience for me. I was determined to hear Him and get my own deliverance so that I would not destroy the church or ministry that God assigned my husband to.

What is my ministry? God has anointed me for business. From as far back as I can remember I always saw myself running my own business. I can recall at the age of 20, during a Bible Study class, my first pastor asking me what I wanted to do with my life. I said as confidently as I could, "I want to get my Bachelors, my Masters, and then my PhD in business." He then spoke into my life that one day I would be running a company. I've always known what I was called to do. Just as my husband studies and gets revelation from the word of God and it excites him, I feel that exact same way when it comes to business. It's who I am and it's what revitalizes me and gives me energy. I can walk into any business and provide you with an evaluation on staff, finances, and who needs to be terminated in order for your business to grow without you even filling me in on your company. It's a gift that God blessed me with and it's one that has always been with me from my first job until now as a business owner. It's my ministry! Some people refer to it as "Marketplace Ministry." Whatever you may call it, that's what excites me.

My ministry (in the marketplace) is to employ those who need some assistance, training, mentoring, and mothering. So it goes beyond just finances or profit and loss statements. Now once I have done what God has spoken to me to do, then it's up to the person to take care of the information and gifts that God has given them. It's out of my hands at that point because it's not my doing anyway, it's God's doing.

Chapter Nine

Business Naysayers

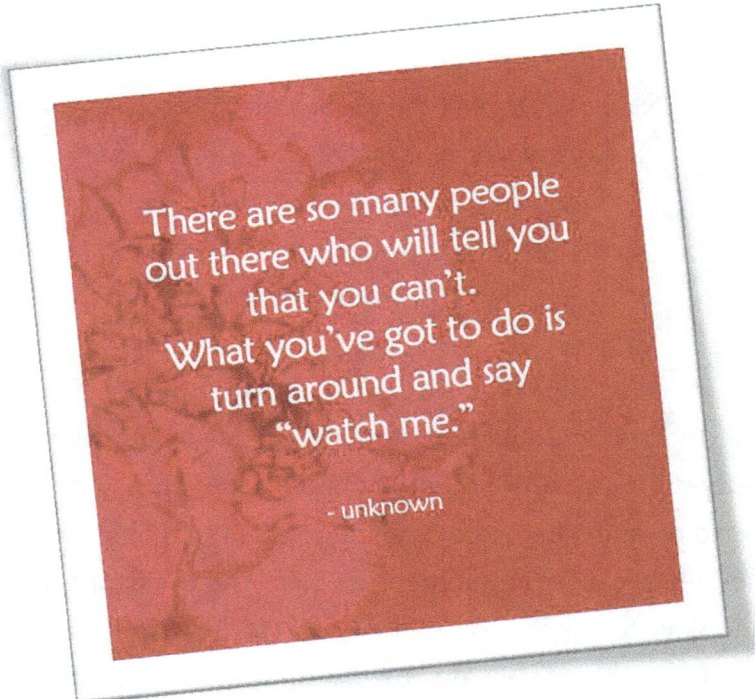

> There are so many people out there who will tell you that you can't.
> What you've got to do is turn around and say "watch me."
>
> - unknown

I heard a great statement from one of our dear friends in the faith, Dr. Leon Crawford. He was visiting our home once and we were discussing church and he made this statement:

"Who has your keys?
Do they have keys to your house?
Do they have keys to your car?
Do they have keys to your office?
Do they have keys to your church?
Do they have keys to your business?

Now ask yourself this, "Have they given you any keys to anything they own? Yet they say they love you. Jesus says, "I give you everything that I own – I will give you my keys!" (Paraphrased)

Whenever you aim for success in anything in life, you will have those who doubt your potential and even question your motives. It's okay if you are confident in whom God called you to be and what He called you to do. I'm thankful for my enemies because they sometimes force me to fast, pray, and seek God for direction. Nobody would have ever believed that I would become the owner of a successful childcare center, helping my husband run a ministry, and overseeing our café. I would have never believed that I would be writing grants for not only our own nonprofit but for other nonprofit organizations as well. The word of God says that a good man's steps are ordered by the Lord and I am totally convinced that my steps are ordered by Him.

Chapter Nine - Business Naysayers

God has truly anointed me for business and I also believe that He uses people in the marketplace who can teach others to walk in integrity and honor as they serve Him. I love my walk and although there are days that are harder than others, I'm still appreciative for what I have.

So what if most of our friends don't support our businesses or even say, "Congratulations?" I've learned to be okay with it, because God still blesses us and still moves in the midst of any discomfort. I've learned that if you want success it will cost you something and if you want growth it will require a measure of pain.

Sometimes, better yet, the majority of the time, you cannot wait for friends to support you. You have to continue to trust God and walk in what He has called you to. For me being in the field I'm in and with my level of expertise, there are still people who sit right in our church who will go outside the church to seek counsel concerning how to start a business or operate a business – and will even pay for it. Yet, I'm right there in the house of the Lord with them and sometimes I'm even willing to do it for free. Now don't get me wrong, once I know you have gone outside and paid someone money…well, guess what? You got it. You will pay me, too.

I use to feel guilty about the way I run my businesses because everyone does not believe in my style of management. One night I went to a women's ministry at one of my friends' church and she told me so clearly, "Don't you dare allow anyone to hinder what God has done for you. They don't know the sacrifices you made; how you borrowed money from your 401K to start your business and how you've had to make sure payroll gets done, give people job opportunities, so on and so forth. Yet they want to dictate to you how to run your business. Don't let these soothsayers hinder you! And some of them are just jealous anyway." My husband would say that you're not really blessed or favored of the Lord if you don't have any people envious of you. Bring on the haters, it's just an indicator of how blessed you are.

    I am a woman of God who owns businesses and I refuse to allow antagonizing voices to dictate to me how to run that business. My attitude is that if they don't like the way I run my business they can go start their own. Is that being arrogant? No. It's just truth. And it has helped me to safeguard and grow my businesses. Don't get me wrong, there are people who support me 100% and would do anything for me as I would them. I take constructive criticism from those who have my best interest at heart. I wrote this to encourage that young entrepreneur who has been told they won't be successful or they shouldn't busy themselves in pursuing after their dream. If God told you to do it and has anointed you for it, I say "Go wholeheartedly towards fulfilling your destiny and your call to the marketplace." I've learned that only devils attempt to hinder the plan of God.

Chapter Nine - Business Naysayers

Let your naysayers make you more determined to manifest your God-given dream.

Chapter Ten
I'm Grateful for it All

   As I sit on the airplane the pilot comes in and says, "We are in our final descent into sunny Orlando." I peep out the window and cannot help but remember how blessed my life is. I began to reflect on the best and worst moments of my life that have brought me to where I am today. My husband

and I are about to land in sunny Florida for a few days of rest and relaxation (I hope – with him you never know because he's so mission-minded). I smile on the inside because I'm grateful for what God has done in my life. I'm thankful for the path He has allowed my feet to travel. I would have never imagined that I could ever be married again, this time to the man of my dreams for over 23 years now, through Social Service help, bankruptcies and financial woes and now at a place of owning my own business, becoming financially secure, driving the car of my preference when we used to have less than stellar vehicles, and going from Section 8 apartments to homeownership in our beautiful home. I'm grateful. The Lord has blessed me with four amazing grandchildren, a God-fearing daughter-in-law and son who love God, a church family who we are able to serve and reciprocate the same back to us and have built great relationships.

I'm finally at a point in my life that I am embracing what God has done for me and not having any regrets. The Father deserves my praise, not merely for what He has done for me materially, because honestly, He gave me the strength and ability to achieve material success without fear and doubt. But what I praise Him for is that after all the hell I have been through in my life I honestly and wholeheartedly want to serve Him. I almost gave up! I almost threw in the towel, but He comforted me and shielded me and infused His strength in me and forgave me of ALL my sins and gave me a second chance. He deserves my utmost worship.

After living on this earth for over fifty years, you begin to reflect on what you could have done better, mistakes you've made, and choices that turned out to be wrong. I don't think I would change anything about my life, which some of you will never understand. I am who I am today because of my life experiences. I didn't read a book to get here or attend a seminar to follow certain steps; I simply applied the word of God, prayed as much as possible, held on to God's unchanging hand, supported my husband, loved on my family, and gave of myself unconditionally.

My life is my life and I love it!

Conclusion

I have learned that over the 38 years that I have been saved that 'people are people' and many will always do what's best for themselves and for their own interest. I have personal goals and things I want to achieve but I also want to see God's will performed in my life as well as those around me, so I try not to put my self-interest in front of God's interest for my life. The Scripture is so true, "Delight yourself in the Lord and He will give you the desires of your heart" (Psalm 37:4).

This book was not a tell-all-your-secrets book, although I did reveal quite a bit about my past. I hope that it was encouragement to you as it was a blessing for me to share from some of my life experiences. I wanted you to know that though I love Jesus with all my being, I can say with transparency that I occasionally have to confess when I get lost, stumble and fall along the way. I declare to you that I am nothing without Him. I can't even begin to imagine how I survived all that I have without His grace. It lets me know that I have strength within me that I didn't even realize was there. Because of what the Lord has done in me and for me, I have no regrets. As a matter of fact, I celebrate me, Barbara, today for accomplishing something that was prophesied to me over 25 years ago. I know that this book is the first of many books that the Lord has placed in me. I want to take this time to say a simple prayer to God. And you may pray a similar prayer to Him as well:

"Thanks again, Daddy God, for entrusting your presence with me and entrusting the two wonderful children you gave to my care. I thank You, Daddy, for forgiving me of the mistakes I made and for the trials that I had to face because they have made me the woman I am today. Thank You for trusting my heart to the king I share my life with because I know at times I don't deserve him, but I'm grateful anyway. I honor You for those women who are honestly there for me and not intimidated by my God-given gifts or my call. I honor You for allowing me to experience true friendships and knowing what that feels like. Thank You, Adonai, for trusting me to employ people and teach others how to do the same. I thank You, Father, that You did not allow me to succumb to the howling voices of negativity concerning me, threats from the enemy in sheep clothing, nor from the opinions of others who thought they were better than me or that I was undeserving of your blessings and favor. You are my God and it is in You that I put my trust. I thank you that when I call upon your name you hear me and answer me. Words are never enough to tell you how much I adore and appreciate the unique way you created me. You created me as an original and You remind me that I'm the

Conclusion

only me in the world and after me you broke the mold. Lord, thank you for saving me from myself and helping me to love myself and affording me the privilege to be a blessing to others. For this I give you praise, honor and glory. In the matchless name of Jesus Christ, I pray. Amen"

Now, it is time for you to be celebrated as your journey of regrouping and recovery from life's tragedies and hurts begins. The same Lord who helped me will help you, too. He has no respect of persons. He promises to help all those who come to Him with a broken and contrite heart (Psalm 34:18). He says that if we draw near to Him that He will draw near unto us (James 4:8). I encourage you to run to Him and yield your life to Him, all of your feelings, all of your pain and hurt, all of your insecurities, fears and doubts, give it to the Master. He is calling you out of darkness and into His marvelous light (1 Peter 2:9). There is so much to life than tragedy and loss. There is so much to life than pain and misfortune. Jesus has come to give us life and to give it to us more abundantly (John 10:10b). May the Lord our God bless you real good.

References:

Recommended Resource: Suicide: A Christian Response : Five Crucial Considerations for Choosing Life by Gary Stewart.

11 facts about suicide. Do something.org. Retrieved from: https://www.dosomething.org/us/facts/11-facts-about-suicide

About the Author

Barbara has worked in the non-profit sector and currently operates a childcare center (Kingdom Kare, Inc.) and café (Kingdom Kafe and Lounge) along with her husband.

She has traveled extensively abroad visiting such countries as Germany, Scotland, England, Kenya, Israel and Italy. She holds a Bachelor's degree in Bank Finance, a Bachelor's degree in Divinity and a Master's degree in Pastoral Counseling; she is currently working on her degree in Early Childhood Education-Administration and Psychology.

She has served on the State of Maryland's Department of Juvenile Services Advisory Board for female juvenile offenders, the Anne Arundel County Suicide Prevention Advisory Board for the public school system, and is a member of the National Association of Professional Women. She has been listed in Who's Who among International Executive Women and has received a Governor's Citation for her work with youth in the community.

Barbara is currently COO (Chief Operating Officer) of Kingdom Kare, Inc. which consists of a childcare center, Mentor programs, and parenting workshops. In addition, Barbara works alongside her husband as Lead Pastor of

Kingdom Celebration Center in Odenton, Maryland. She enjoys spending quality time with her family – her son, daughter-in-law and four grandchildren.

www.ingramcontent.com/pod-product-compliance
Lightning Source LLC
Chambersburg PA
CBHW070548300426
44113CB00011B/1822